Investing

Learn How To Be The Most Effective Landlord To Maximize Your Investment Returns

(Fundamentals Of Stock Market Investing For Wealth)

Marcelo Jacobs

TABLE OF CONTENT

How Much Capital Is Necessary To Get Started? 1

Take Charge Of Your Financial Situation 7

Investing Vs. Working 23

Cryptocurrencies, The Metaverse, Non-Fungible Tokens, And The Future 33

How To Evaluate Airbnb Rental Properties..............42

Functioning Of The Metaverse 51

Shares/Stocks/Equities...76

Everyone Can Improve Their Investment Skills. 92

Effectiveness Of Passive Income................................. 101

The Issue With Savings Accounts................................ 114

Missteps To Avoid.. 125

How Much Capital Is Necessary To Get Started?

There is no minimum investment amount, but it appears legitimate that you must commence with a few hundred dollars to generate a profit.

Certain investments will have a minimum amount, so always consult with your financial advisor to determine the ideal amount for your situation.

You should also consider the amount of money you are willing to invest. There is always an element of risk, and you should only contribute what you can afford to lose.

Never invest money that you cannot afford to lose. The key is to build up your reserve funds prior to making contributions. Thus, you will have the means to cope with adversities such as job loss or illness.

You should not save money you need to fulfill other obligations.

Consider the Long Term

When you invest, you anticipate greater returns than you would receive from a bank account, but you must confess that you intend to hold your investments for the longer term. Thus, you provide them with the greatest opportunity to reach their destination.

Share prices fluctuate, so a longer holding period affords a greater opportunity for positive events to offset the declines from a bad period.

Being a long-term investor as opposed to a transient merchant enables you to profit from recognizing issues and negotiating solutions. Become increasingly financially astute.

The longer the holding period, the lower the probability of calamity as the base normal return rises.

Investing in the stock market will not result in instantaneous wealth.

Investing in the financial market is a slow, consistent, and reliable method of accumulating wealth. With a normal annual growth rate of 7%, your underlying speculation will double in ten years; however, this will not occur immediately.

The stock market is one of the most effective wealth-building tools available, but you must adhere to a few principles.

You need to know exactly what you are investing in, keep an eye on your expenses, build a diversified portfolio, and contribute for as long as possible if you need the most apparent opportunity to accumulate wealth.

Independent Research

You should understand what you are investing in and how it operates. You can still utilize a financial advisor's services, but it is always preferable to familiarize yourself with everything first.

If you are interested in investing in a specific organization, you should investigate its issues. You can review their financial reports and any other available information about them.

Before undertaking any endeavor, you should conduct your own research.

There are publicly accessible data sources for virtually every industry. The annual report of an organization provides a sufficient overview of the business as well as projections for its future growth.

You can also favor exchange magazines and websites that cater to a particular industry.

Focus on the organization's strengths and weaknesses. Understanding the financial soundness of a company is the most important step in stock analysis.

Learn how to interpret a company's asset report, pay explanation, and income statements.

By learning more about finance, you will realize that you should never blindly accept what stock analysts say, as you should always conduct your own research.

Take Charge Of Your Financial Situation

At some point in your existence, you should pause and evaluate your financial situation. Is it true that you are exactly where you should be? Is it true that you are struggling to earn a living wage and have no idea how you'll be able to meet the long-term responsibilities of your home loan, school obligations, and inevitable retirement? Allow me to assure you that the majority of the people you know have been or are currently in a similar situation. After leaving home, becoming financially independent as well as secure and stable is a difficult path to navigate, unless you were born into the world already privileged beyond belief.

One way to assume responsibility for your financial situation is to invest in pay delivering land while continuing to work at your current job and saving your current income source, however unassuming it may be.

Before embarking on your journey to financial security, you should assess your current financial situation and make whatever improvements you can in a reasonable amount of time. Developing your reliability further is a crucial step. You are not required to fulfill all of your obligations and maintain an excellent FICO score. Obviously, these would help, but there are some consistent steps you can take in a relatively short period of time that will improve your financial well-being and overall creditworthiness.

Compute the Balance Sheet

Once you have decided to increase your financial well-being, one of the first steps you must take is to assess your current financial situation. Creating a financial record and a pay and cost document is the most effective method for achieving this objective.

A financial accounting report is a budget summary that summarizes your current assets and liabilities. It has several distinct sides or columns:

Assets vs. Liabilities

These two metrics will determine what you own (resources) and what you owe (liabilities) and provide a solid understanding of your current financial situation.

Each page of the accounting report will contain sections detailing the value of various assets. On the asset side of the balance sheet are things you own, such as cash and property, while the liability side displays what you owe, such as credit card debt and your mortgage.

This fundamental sheet is accurate and simple to comprehend for the novice, regular financial backer. It is a remarkable representation of your current financial standing. Please note that a financial report does not include your salary. I will elaborate on this topic later.

To create a financial record, list your current liquid and fixed assets alongside your current liabilities. Below is an example of a monetary record:

To determine your total assets, you subtract what you owe from what you claim.

The fluid resources are a significant factor that has yet to be determined and are also significant. Typically, purchasing land requires financial resources. While in Chapter 8 I will discuss methods for purchasing land without a large quantity of capital, this will be more of an exception than the norm. In addition, the more liquid resources you have, the more secure any land venture will be.

The difference between a successful investment in real estate and one that ends in failure could be having a few thousand dollars in the bank to tide you over during an opportunity, unexpected repair, or other obstacle. Some moneylenders do not require a minimum of six months of home loan payments for potential future use. Always reserve some funds for your insurance, regardless of whether you are using a credit extension, overdraft, or credit card. As with everything else in ordinary life, Murphy's Law frequently becomes the most significant factor, and you will discover the need for specific supplies. In every circumstance, it is preferable to prepare for the worst rather than be blindsided by life's intangibles.

Create a Profit and Loss Statement

The second sheet I mentioned that you would need to prepare is a pay and expense sheet, which can give you a crucial understanding of where your money comes from and goes. Essentially, this is a written spending schedule. As you add properties to your portfolio, you must account for their costs and pay for them.

Most loan specialists prefer a stable income. Generally, they will allow you to use approximately 44% of your constant income to pay for home loans and other expenses. I will investigate how banks typically convert rental income to successful income in a later section.

You should always be aware of how much money is available each month for savings and investments. Since you should only acquire properties that generate a profit, your disposable income will increase with each property you acquire. Assuming you were already generating a decent living prior to the investment property purchase, the addition of pay will essentially increase your income.

Below is an example of a pay and expenditure worksheet for an individual.

Note that the two segment totals are equivalent. This is because you regularly deposit extra income into your bank account. (Here, it is $200, and it is displayed as an expenditure.) If your expenses are greater than your income, you need to make adjustments.

Repay Debts

This should be self-evident, but you wouldn't believe how frequently it is ignored or neglected. Take care of your responsibilities! Assuming you truly wish to increase your income, fulfill your obligations. If you wish to improve your ratio of income to obligations, you should eliminate your debt.

The two most important things you can do to improve your FICO score are to pay your expenses on time and to avoid maxing out your credit cards and other lines of credit. Even if you have paid all of your expenses on time, if your Visas are maxed out, your credit score may not be all that great. If you pay these off, even to 90 percent (or less, if possible), it will improve your FICO score and free up credit for emergencies.

This will be examined in greater depth later in the chapter.

Good Debt Verses Bad Debt

I will tell you something that may surprise you... I am thousands of dollars in the negative. Is that dreadful? not even remotely! My obligation is one of "great obligation." I used cash to purchase land that generates income and positive cash flow!

Visas, vehicles, yachts, RVs, and your mortgage are examples of dreadful obligations. You may wonder why your mortgage is listed as a poor obligation. Essentially, it does not generate income or pay for itself. Even though the largest asset most Americans possess is their residence, it is not a significant obligation. To generate income from your property, you must sell it. Most of us don't anticipate selling our homes, so it's not a huge undertaking, but it can be a source of low-income funds to help you get started.

Good obligations include contracts for land speculation, business advances, and credit extensions. These are used to employ assets and generate income.

It is the dreadful obligation that you wish to eliminate!

The advance on your own home is the least expensive source of funds in terms of financing costs that you pay. This is the least costly cash available.

Lenders are acutely aware that the last item a person will give up is their home. In addition, land values routinely increase, so a mortgage is generally a sure thing for moneylenders. There are risks associated with transporting currency out of your home, as doing so puts your residence at risk.

You can obtain modest funds from your residence for land donation. For instance, you can renegotiate your mortgage and receive cash at a 5% premium, which you can then prudently invest in other land and earn a return of at least 30%. This is intelligent investing, but you must always remember that your home is at risk. This is not a wise financial decision if you borrow against your property in order to take a vacation or purchase a larger vehicle. You want your home to complete tasks on your behalf. If it will not directly generate income because you are not selling or renting it, its inherent value must be put to use in other ways. Purchasing your property and reinvesting the proceeds in "great obligation" will enable you to utilize the value of your home in a financially prudent manner.

Short-, middle-, and long-term savings

Before purchasing your first investment property, you should have a financial reserve. Assuming you purchase the property via a conventional moneylender, this will be a requirement. They must be certain that even if the property is vacant or has other issues for a couple of months, you will continue to make the mortgage payments. However, not all investment properties are acquired through conventional channels. As I will discuss in Chapter 8, there are a variety of land-buying strategies that require little or no capital. However, I will never recommend purchasing land without adequate reserves.

True domestic contribution involves controlled risk. It is essentially as dangerous as you allow it to be. What will you do if a tenant damages your investment property and you need to pay for repairs if you have no cash in your checking account, investment funds, or other accounts? Not only will this substantially increase pressure, but it could also result in the loss of your property.

I frequently use the expression, "prepare for the worst, but hope for the best." This is accomplished by ensuring that I have a half-year's worth of stocks in a fluid or semi-fluid record. I should acknowledge that, comparable to some first-time investors, this was not always true for me. When I first began, I did not have enough funds to cover a half-year of expenses. I had almost no resources, and my total assets were actually negative. I had nothing to lose by attempting, so I accepted the challenge. I would not recommend this to everyone, but I was unwilling to wait a few more years to release my holdings. The good news is that I did have some available credit on a few credit cards that I could have used in an emergency. Does this seem like you? I would never suggest staking your entire work on a hunch that has no certainty for advancement, but in my circumstance, a change is necessary. I did not need to continue halting my life at this time; however, I did need to continue living it!

If you choose the prudent path, which is plainly advised, you must begin saving while simultaneously paying off your enormous debt. The most effective method for achieving this is to start early and consistently save money. You should have cash in both your financial records and your investment account. If at all possible, commence contributing funds to a common asset account. You will be astonished at how quickly these accounts grow if you diligently manage monthly deposits into each of the three accounts. Your common asset record can be an IRA, which provides some tax advantages. Some lenders prefer not to consider a retirement account as part of your reserves, but you can frequently persuade them that you could and would withdraw funds from the account if necessary. Assuming you begin investing 5% of your pay into the common asset, as the scale of your venture properties increases, so will the number of your stores. It is that easy!

Investing Vs. Working

As individuals begin to participate in land investment, the amount of labor that will be required for a random investment strategy may be the most obscure element to new investors.

Let's differentiate between contributing and working.

Investing: currency is the vehicle for profit

Working: effort is the means to success

With stocks, you give over your money, do nothing other than possibly occasionally check the stock prices, and then eventually withdraw your money. The money you earn from your corporate securities is pure speculation. You perform no labor, so each benefit is a result of the speculation itself.

Investing in land notes is comparable to this. You invest funds in the note without performing any labor, so any profit you make on the investment is a direct result of the speculation itself.

The majority of people enter land contributing to accomplish the same thing — an endeavor. They are seeking a return on their investment. They must invest a certain amount of cash in a business venture or opportunity, and they must receive additional cash as a return. In general, this is how a speculation works, and it is reasonable to assume that this is what individuals hope to achieve by investing in land.

However, things can go awry when people don't realize that some land investment strategies require a ridiculous amount of labor. Work is not something terrible, but it is not identical to investing.

In the case of certain land investment strategies, your investment return is directly proportional to the amount of effort you put forth. If you invest time and effort into a venture, you will receive a combination of 1) investment and 2) compensation for your time and effort (labor). Consider the property trading example. You acquire a distressed property and its recovery. This is your financial endeavor. However, at that point you recover the property on your own. You spend time repairing and enhancing objects and supervising contracted laborers. Suppose you devote 200 hours to the rehabilitation of this property over the course of four months. Assuming you are telling the truth about the profit you make on the reversal, you would consider a portion of that profit to be compensation for the 200 hours you spent on the project and the remainder to be the actual profit from the investment, rather than considering the entire amount to be profit from the investment.

It's important to identify the source of your financial gain because a) you want to ensure that you're earning your target amount on your investment and b) you need to know in advance how much time and effort this particular investment will require in order to determine whether you can realistically do it or not.

Every business system will require a different amount of labor. To give you some ideas, here are the most well-known land speculation strategies:

Wholesaling: work without investment

half effort and half investment are required for a successful reversal.[8]

Investing in rental properties entails half effort and half profit

Using property managers for rental properties involves negligible effort and primarily financial investment.

REITs and notes: no effort, all investment

Again, what is the significance of this? Since you must weigh the consequences of laboring for your ventures against:

✓ expertise level premium level ✓ ✓ availability hazard tolerances ✓

Personally, I have a great deal of access and risk tolerance to be able to engage in wild speculation. My expertise level is not terrible, but not great either; I'm bad at doing specialized work myself, but I'm great at project management, so I could supervise contract employees if necessary. My disadvantage, however, lies in my advantage level. To say I have absolutely no advantage in coping with my speculations would be an understatement. I'm dissatisfied, I don't enjoy supervising project workers, I try to avoid waking up early to meet project workers, I like to work as little as possible for money, and I dislike being secured or required to be somewhere at a specific time.

When I observe this level of vigilance, I am better able to determine which venture strategies may be optimal for me. This evaluation will be unique for each individual, and it is your responsibility to be honest with yourself.

Otherwise, you may quickly develop a dislike for your investments.

Investing IS NOT Wholesaling

Wholesale is one of the most well-known land investment systems presented to amateur investors. You engage in wholesaling when you, as a distributor, identify exceptional speculation deals and deliver them to financial backers; you then earn money by marking up the price to the financial backer. For example, you observe a home selling for $50,000 and a speculator willing to pay $55,000 for it. By administering administrative tasks and acting as an intermediary, you are able to maintain the difference between the two costs; this is your profit.

Appears to be sufficiently straightforward, yes?

Wholesale is advantageous in a variety of ways. It can teach incredible real estate investing skills such as mathematics, deal-finding, negotiating, and networking. Additionally, it requires little to no initial investment, so anyone can do it. It can even be lucrative. While it's not always as easy to get into wholesaling as it's often advertised to be, it's a basic business that you can do on your own and with as much creativity as you wish.

However, now comes the unpleasant awakening. The strategy of wholesaling is advocated similarly to that of speculation. Not even remotely is wholesaling a form of conjecture.

Wholesale is 100 percent labor and zero percent speculation. Perhaps you spent a few dollars on flyers or advertising for properties, but this is unquestionably an investment in your wholesaling business.

Wholesaling is labor. Assuming you take up wholesaling, you've taken up a duty. Accepting a new position is acceptable so long as it is a task you were already intending to undertake. In the not too distant future, you may have the choice to create frameworks and cycles for your wholesaling business and hire people to complete the work on your behalf, thereby making it a less time-consuming endeavor. It involves running a business. If you're as of now working 60 hours per week and have a group of five and you want to get into land contributing, you'll need to get that if you choose to discount that you're taking on a second job instead of contributing, which may not be a practical option given your full schedule.

Wholesaling can be a great way to build capital to invest in real estate, and it can teach you a great deal about investing. However, you can also build capital by taking on a second job, obtaining loans, selling items on eBay, or starting a different type of business, which may be of greater interest to you. I don't want to burst the bubble that wholesaling is the easiest method for someone with no money to start investing, but it's not.

Cryptocurrencies, The Metaverse, Non-Fungible Tokens, And The Future

It's no secret that the Metaverse is the next big event that will occur in our society. It would revolutionize the world as we currently know it and offer unfathomable possibilities for present and future generations.

The Metaverse is intended to create a platform where physical presence-required events can be attended regardless of physical distance. We participate virtually, but not in the same manner as video calls and conferences. You will be represented by your preferred avatar and will be able to engage in virtual handshakes, hugs, and property excursions.

The NFTs are a peculiar aspect of the Metaverse. Consider what purchasing avatars will be like. It will be comparable to purchasing stock trousers from a boutique.

Gaming and the Metaverse will provide the blockchain with genuine utility. People will continue to play games and watch their Metaverse show even when the price of Bitcoin is falling. Some people won't bother about coin price; all they want to do in the Metaverse is play games and communicate with their loved ones.

Businesses are beginning to adopt a virtual presence. You will not need to travel to accomplish certain objectives.

Although there will always be a connection between the online and offline worlds, it is possible to acquire items from the online world and receive them offline.

You can purchase items from virtual stores and use them virtually, depending on the purchase.

You can purchase an eBook digitally and choose to read it in a tranquil setting. Simply access the eBook seller's virtual store, purchase the book, select any live background theme you desire, and start reading. There will be businesses offering premium backgrounds for a fee, or you can select from the free options.

You can accomplish all of these without exiting your room.

The value is where the money is.

In the virtual world, one can construct a unique game home that entices gamers from around the world to pay for access to their virtual game environments. This will enhance the value of this virtual property, which you can then sell to the highest bidder while the owner receives the funds offline.

There will be houses and streets with moving virtual individuals, as well as billboards for advertisements. You may purchase Ad spaces to promote your products on virtual streets.

As we speak, individuals are already purchasing land at a discount in order to sell it to you at a higher price when you awake.

Remember that the government will also enter, and you will be required to pay tax there.

There is more to this Metaverse, but this post is already sufficiently lengthy. I will shortly publish additional in-depth posts on this subject, and yes, we are already developing a blockchain-based product that will profit from this Metaverse in the near future.

Manifestations of the Metaverse

Creators of crypto metaverses have frequently sought to distinguish their domains from previous iterations of metaverses in three crucial ways:

Decentralization: In contrast to earlier digital environments, which were managed and owned by corporations, crypto metaverses are frequently democratic, with all or some metaverse gaming aspects utilizing the blockchain framework. Therefore, blockchain-based metaverses appear to deviate from the mainstream corporate frameworks and value exploitation strategies of the modern gaming industry. The unique characteristics of blockchain-based games can provide participants with fairer participation options. Additionally, it implies that the Metaverse's inhabitants share ownership. In the unlikely event that the original designers of the metaverse blockchain abandoned the project, the game could remain intact indefinitely.

Governance tokens and DAOs (Decentralized autonomous organizations) are used by crypto metaverses such as Decentraland to place their players in control of the game's future by allowing them to vote on modifications and upgrades. In this way, metaverses may develop into complete communities with democratic governance and economies, transcending their status as merely cryptocurrency-based games.

Verifiable Provenance: In crypto metaverses, cryptocurrency tokens, such as NFTs, are used as in-world commodities. In gaming environments, purchases and achievements can be quite valuable to participants. Non-fungible tokens modernize in-game product standards by providing asset marketplaces with much-needed transparency and accessibility. As each non-fungible token is unique, Metaverse coins and items can be easily programmed to authenticate the source of user-guaranteed in-game content and non-fungible token gaming resources.

Since crypto metaverses utilize blockchain technology and cryptocurrencies, their economics are intrinsically linked to the broader crypto industry. The actual value of metaverse currencies, digital real estate, and avatar costumes can now be traded on NFT exchanges and other decentralized exchanges.

How To Evaluate Airbnb Rental Properties

You want to purchase an Airbnb as an investment property, but you're stuck on how to analyze a prospective purchase. If so, this section is what you need to read, as it explains in detail how to determine whether or not a property will generate income as an Airbnb. We will select a property presently listed on the MLS and provide an example of how we analyze properties in the real world. This instruction will now utilize a custom Airbnb analysis calculator. You can either create it yourself or download it.

When analyzing a property on Airbnb, there are two primary categories to consider. The first category is the property's income, and the second is its expenses. There are subcategories within the categories, and we will examine these subcategories in depth. Let's begin with the first category.

Category One The income from the property

When analyzing a conventional long-term rental, it is relatively simple to project the income. It will be the same amount each month for the length of time specified in the lease between the proprietor and tenant. Suppose, as a landlord, you sign a 12-month lease with your tenant, and the tenant agrees to pay

$1000 per month. Then, you can rely on receiving $1000 per month, assuming your lessee pays on time.

Short-term rentals are a separate industry. The income fluctuates greatly from month to month and day to day. There is no rent being paid, no lease being signed, and no tenant.

Short-Term Leases

With short-term rentals, you have guests instead of tenants, and instead of long-term leases where your property is entirely occupied for the duration of the lease, your guests check in for a brief period of time, typically a few days. The percentage of the year that your property will be unoccupied due to no reservations is known as the occupancy rate. As we progress through the book, we will delve a little deeper.

Rather than paying a fixed monthly rent, your visitors pay a daily rate to stay at your property, which varies from day to day and month to month. In summary, your short-term rental income is determined by:

The average daily rate that your visitors pay to stay at your establishment.

The frequency with which your hotel is scheduled is known as its occupancy rate.

Since I purchased my miniature Mojave home eight months ago, it has averaged 85 occupants per day at an average daily rate of $188. When analyzing a short-term rental, you must also include housekeeping fees in the income.

Cleaning Costs

If a cleaning fee is something you pay to your cleaning staff, you may wonder why you should count it as income. Now, there are two motivations for doing this.

The first step to becoming an Airbnb host is to charge a cleaning fee to your visitors. This means that when Airbnb deposits funds into your account, they deposit the total of the nightly rate plus the cleaning fee. You receive the sum of these numbers.

You should also include the cleaning fee in your income because, as a host, you can make a modest profit from it. What exactly do I mean by this? You pay your cleaner $150 each time they clean your property, but the cleaning fee you charge your clients is $175. This results in a profit of $25 each time your property is cleansed.

$25 may not seem like much, but if you turn your property over 15 times per month, that's an additional $375 per month or $4,500 per year from the cleaning fee alone. This can help cover expenses such as purchasing toilet paper, towels, soap, and other amenities for your visitors. An additional $375 per month, which is equivalent to almost purchasing a long-term rental elsewhere, is included in the cleaning fee. In summary, your Airbnb income is determined by the average daily rate, the occupancy rate, and the cleaning fees.

Category Two

The second category is comprised of Airbnb-related expenses. There are numerous costs to consider, so let's run through this list rapidly.

The accommodation cost must be factored into your monthly principal, interest, tax, and insurance payment.

Utility expense

You must consider your utility costs, unlike in a long-term rental where the tenant pays the majority, if not all, of the utility costs. As the proprietor or host of a short-term rental, you are solely responsible for all utility costs. This includes the costs of water, electricity, gas, garbage, cable, and the internet.

Cleaning Costs

The following cost is your cleaning charge. The cleaning fee should also be included in your expenses, as you must eventually pay the employees who are maintaining your property. Therefore, only the cleaning charge appears as both an income and an expense.

Airbnb Fee

After housekeeping fees, there are Airbnb fees to consider. Listing your property on these websites incurs a fee. They charge American hosts 3% of the total amount paid by visitors. Therefore, you must include this as an expense for the property.

Improvements and Maintenance

Additionally, you must set aside funds for restorations and maintenance. I recommend setting aside between 5 and 10 percent of your gross revenue for restorations and maintenance.

Functioning Of The Metaverse

The metaverse is both a fascinating and controversial phenomenon, as is often the case when something that is not completely prepared for evident technological and experiential limitations is burdened with excessive expectations.

The metaverse was the dominant media phenomenon in 2021, when literature spread like wildfire describing what many consider to be the Internet's designated successor. Because we are naturally enthusiastic about technology and the future, we embarked on a voyage of discovery that we would like to share with you.

Between science-fictional hints and more real-world occurrences than ever before, we will investigate this new dimension in all its forms, attempting to identify its foundational technologies.

The metaverse is currently definable with certainty due to the fact that it does not currently exist.

The CEO of Epic Games, Tim Sweeney, states. "It is clear that none of us knows precisely what the metaverse will be. There are numerous suggestions, and we can understand various aspects of them now, but they existed prior to the emergence of social networks. For the remainder, we are purely improvising and experimenting with hypotheses [...] I believe that the metaverse can be a real-time 3D social media in which we do not exchange communications asynchronously, but instead find ourselves in a virtual world where virtually anything is possible".

The success of the metaverse is likely attributable to its element of mystery, which is capable of eliciting immense anticipation regarding its potential. Imaginative suggestions only serve to amplify this sentiment.

But now it is a matter of doing it, the metaverse, and the commitment that lies ahead is far from negligible, as Tim Sweeney correctly notes: "Unlike what we see in certain films, the metaverse cannot be the outcome of a single mega corporation. To generate value through the experiences that users will be able to live in the metaverse, the creative efforts of millions of people will be required to build platforms, content, programming, and design.

The metaverse of today is a multibillion dollar industry comprised of online games, virtual concerts, fashion collections, and blockchain-based NFTs.

We haven't been able to discover a convincing definition of the metaverse, but we're not giving up! We will alter our strategy, pursuing a different line of inquiry, in order to determine the characteristics of the contexts that are presently classified as commercial metaverses.

In the magical world of the Internet, the term metaverse is frequently associated with situations exhibiting the following characteristics, as noted by The Verge in a variety of contexts:

3D virtual worlds and avatar customization,

Diverse interpersonal interactions that are less competitive than traditional multiplayer gaming.

Existence of "user-generated content" logic, in which users can create the original contents that populate virtual worlds, such as accessories for customizing avatars, constructions, interior design, and event organization.

Systems for monetizing user-generated content,

Businesses that create branded content and events to promote their products within virtual world communities.

Creating immersive experiences with virtual reality and augmented reality technology.

Life simulator

Virtual worlds in 3D that are a complete alternative to the real world, in which you can construct your own headquarters and residence, dress your avatars, and do everything else necessary to guarantee the social interactions of an online community.

Second Life (2003), which experienced its golden years in the 2000s, when millions of users populated its virtual world and generated a thriving economy related to personalized content, remains the most prominent example. Numerous brands have implemented a marketing strategy involving the placement of their products and the coordination of in-game events due to Second Life's popularity.

Multiplayer video games

In contrast to the traditional definition of competitive multiplayer, some games emphasize the construction of a community within the platform, where social interaction between participants is possible. The most relevant example is Fortnite, the popular battle royale game by Epic Games, whose community has become a point of reference for in-game events sponsored by various brands.

Metaverse and gaming platforms

They differ from conventional multiplayer games in that users can generate and share content with almost complete freedom.

In this context, Minecraft and Roblox are the most well-known platforms, with a combined valuation of close to 50 billion dollars. Its audience is comprised of children between 8 and 13 years old. Roblox is a very attractive platform for marketing campaigns due to its extremely youthful user base, which attracts numerous brands.

Musical events

Similar to Roblox, Fortnite online concerts can guarantee artists millions of viewers. Especially in light of the current COVID emergency.

Fashion technology

The pandemic has effectively rendered international fashion weeks impossible by eradicating the traditional communication channels of the new collections. The brands have increased their investments in fashion technology, beginning to create online events with 3D virtual catwalks for fashion shows and ad hoc 3D environments to present the new product lines and accessories.

Gucci has announced that, regardless of the pandemic, it will forsake the traditional fashion calendar in order to focus solely on its own events, with which it identifies most strongly. Therefore, the Florentine company has concentrated on the production of virtual events, utilizing NFTs as a new digital distribution channel.

NFT

In reality, the metaverse generates parallel realities that can be experienced through a customized avatar. Customizing the avatar enables the addition of value to digital content, which coincides with the substance of NFT (Non-Fungible Token) tokens, which, through blockchain technology, make it possible to make digital assets unique, otherwise freely reproducible. NFTs may also be acquired and resold via particular platforms.

Metaverse and social Virtual Reality

Social VR employs virtual reality to provide a significantly more immersive experience than conventional social media. Its diffusion is presently quite limited, as it is a relatively new technology, but Microsoft has recently acquired and relaunched VR Chat and Altspace VR, which are already available.

The reality that these 3D environments are distributed via the web currently restricts their graphic capabilities.

Are metaverses really metaverses? The rediscovery and growth of online communities

Whether it's a multiplayer game or a 3D stage where a virtual concert is performed, these applications are designed to keep users online for as long as possible so that content can be sold. But where would the innovation be specifically? It is necessary to contextualize the current evolutionary scenario in an appropriate manner before proceeding.

Fortnite is a prime example. Initiated as a tech prototype for Unreal Engine 4, it languished for years until its developers, riding the success of PUBG, decided to transform it into a battle royale.

The experiential evolution of a product originally created for other purposes has made Fortnite an epoch-defining phenomenon, generating a billion-dollar industry in a very brief period of time. It was what the population desired.

Immersive technologies, the nature of which is absolutely ideal for allowing users to immerse themselves in 3D virtual worlds, are currently generating a great deal of interest but are still only marginally implemented.

Mark Zuckerberg has never concealed his desire to create a metaverse to attract billions of people, the same ones who are currently registered on Facebook, Instagram, and Whatsapp, in order to guarantee business continuity in the web's experiential generation. The first attempts at creating a metaverse were made with Facebook Horizon, a social virtual reality presently in beta.

Zuckerberg intends to transform Facebook into a true metaverse company, but he is aware that doing so will take time and enormous resources, and that the metaverse will have to belong to everyone, as it is inconceivable for a single company to support such an innovative endeavor. A position that is in some respects ambiguous, but is easily understood.

Mark Zuckerberg's company's investments are manifest in Facebook Reality Labs and the Oculus brand, a massive acquisition in the consumer virtual reality market. Facebook has committed approximately ten billion dollars to research on virtual reality and the metaverse in 2021 alone, and has recently announced its intention to expand its research perimeter to the old continent by employing ten thousand researchers in Europe.

It is a strategically well-considered decision that allows Zuckerberg, in one fell swoop, to benefit from the expertise of European universities, to directly understand a market that is radically different from the American market, and to attract new investors.

If Zuckerberg's wager appears audacious and capable of generating very positive employment effects, Joan Donovan stated in a cogent analysis published in the pages of the Washington Post:

"The longer you can maintain a technology that appears novel and fashionable, the longer you can avoid adhering to the norms. While waiting for the government to organize itself by enacting appropriate legislation, you can spend countless years defending yourself against accusations while generating immense revenues.

The objective would be to establish a new wild west, a game that the large tech companies already know well.

Joan Donovan is a researcher who is dedicated to preventing misinformation and manipulation via social media.

In the wake of the Cambridge Analytica scandal, as many as 17 of the most prominent American news outlets have recently begun to publish Facebook Papers, a report of over 10,000 pages compiled primarily by former employees to expose numerous instances of community-harming behavior that the company failed to prevent in order to avoid economic loss.

Facebook would have ignored the fact that religious hatred campaigns were occurring in India, which resulted in over 50 deaths. A particularly grave incident would involve Zuckerberg, who allegedly agreed to a request from the Vietnamese government to censor communications between some activist groups in order to avoid losing its Southeast Asian market.

If such occurrences initially appear to be unrelated to the main theme, we must endeavor to comprehend that in a hypothetical metaverse, which would be significantly more engaging than current social networks, such occurrences could have even more devastating consequences.

On the one hand, it is absolutely necessary to support innovation and the search for new technologies, which are more than legitimate for a private subject. On the other hand, it is absolutely necessary to outline a perimeter of ethical and regulatory action to avoid the speculative matrix that causes people to fall into a real trap, in which the collective interest is unlikely to prevail.

Metaverse technologies: Digital Twin 3D, AR Cloud, and Virtual Reality

The mentioned metaverses involve a vast array of technologies and serve as the foundation for something more ambitious, capable of surpassing the notion of a dystopian world that is completely separate from the real world. The metaverse is destined to evolve in the coexistence of real and virtual content that can represent the entire continuum of realities.

The essential components to enable this metaverse paradigm consist primarily of three 3D technologies that are still well-known but are not yet mature enough to construct virtual worlds with the same level of realism as the one in which we typically live.

Digital Twin 3D

A 3D technology capable of creating the digital model of an entity present in the real world, to interface it through information layers, sensors, and Internet of Things (IoT) systems. A digital twin allows you to acquire information from the physical model to interact with it via digital systems.

When Sweeney says that the creation of metaverse content will require the work of millions of people, he is also referring to the fact that recreating the real world in 3D will require a massive effort in which technology and creativity must converge in shared, capable protocols and positions to ensure an open and interoperable format for the creation of the virtual world's layers.

If every major technology company develops its own proprietary system, such as Microsoft Bing, it will be difficult to locate a reference environment. presently, open-source projects such as

OpenStreetMap lack the level of implementation required to guarantee a solution in this regard.

Mirrorworld is a common term when discussing the digital counterpart of the physical universe.

Flight Simulator, which utilizes a wide range of cloud technologies from Microsoft Azure and Microsoft Bing to allow virtual pilots to fly over incredibly realistic scenarios, is an example of a highly advanced mirrorworld. The play experience developed by the French of Asobo Studios will serve as a pilot project for enterprise applications.

The AR Cloud

Alternately known as spatial computing, it is a cloud-based augmented reality technology that can add persistent digital content to the actual world.

If I create 3D content, such as a teapot, and place it on a real table using an AR Cloud application, it remains there even after I end a work session. When I begin a new session, I will find my augmented reality teapot exactly where I left it, unless another user working on the same project has moved it.

Some AR Cloud applications already exist in the context of collaboration platforms that enable both multi-presence meetings and shared review and design sessions between multiple users. The defining feature of these environments is their hybrid nature, which permits the simultaneous use of traditional, augmented reality, and virtual reality tools.

The main enabling condition for applications based on spatial computing is the proliferation of high-speed, high-bandwidth connections such as 5G. Augmented reality devices are still quite limited from a computational standpoint.

Virtual reality

VR is the only technology that can guarantee the highest level of immersion and presence in the digital experience. Its combination with digital twin and spatial computing makes it possible to guarantee the entire continuum of realities, from the real world to the completely virtual world, with all the intermediate states consisting of the different levels of augmented reality.

It is not yet an extremely prevalent technology.

Oculus is currently the most widespread consumer VR ecosystem due to the commercial success of the Quest 2 viewer, but the so-called killer app has not yet arrived. A killer app is an application capable of exploding the spread of a technology.

The ability to conduct simulations without relying on the physical availability of plants and products, as well as the ability to try risky situations without endangering operators or halting the production line, are factors that make virtual reality particularly popular for training applications in the enterprise.

Shares/Stocks/Equities

Although they are comparative terms, there are distinctions between them.

The term stocks is more inclusive. It represents a share of ownership. Typically, shares represent a portion of responsibility for a particular company.

Stocks are divided into shares; the smallest division of a company's stock is a share. Every share of stock represents an offer to invest in a company. For instance, if a person claims 1% of a company's stock, you can say they have 1% of the company's offer.

Equity represents ownership of an organization's assets minus its liabilities.

Stocks are small units issued by a company that can be bought and traded.

Why do companies provide them? It allows them to raise funds and locate investors.

When you acquire an offer, you acquire a stake in a company and become a shareholder.

You may have a few privileges and benefits as an investor. You could, for instance, deliberate on business matters or receive profit payments.

The dividend payment is a portion of the advantages paid to investors by a company. A company is not required to generate profits. They can be paid on a recurring basis or as a one-time payment.

Shares do not provide a guarantee of profit, and there is risk associated with all investments. Costs may rise or fall.

You can purchase shares on your own or merge your funds with others in a joint venture. This is referred to as a fund.

How long would it be prudent for you to make contributions? Preferably, a considerable amount of time to allow for the passage of time in case you incur a loss due to market fluctuations.

If you can't hold off your cash for that long and require access to it sooner, then offers are probably not the best option for you at this time.

According to the idiom, do not lock up your assets in one location. It is too risky to hold stock in a single company, and if the value of an investment falls, you will lose money.

What are the advantages of stocks?

• You could potentially receive dividends
• They can cover costs • Adaptable

What are the disadvantages of stocks?

• You probably won't get dividends • Risky

• Market cost can fluctuate

As a first-time investor, a safe option for you would be to invest in a stocks&shares Isas. An Isa is a single bank account with securities and dividends. Isas allow you to invest in a variety of investments and funds.

An Isa is the British equivalent of the American IRA.

You can grow your money in two ways with an offer: if the price of the offer increases, you can generate a profit (it will be worth more than when you purchased it), and if the company decides to pay you dividends.

The easiest method to acquire shares is through an online offer management platform. You are able to purchase shares from any company listed on the stock exchange.

You ought to establish a trading account. After opening and funding your account, you are able to purchase equities through the dealer's website.

Other alternatives include using a full-service stockbroker or purchasing shares directly from the company.

How would you select stocks? An excellent place to start is by researching companies you have interacted with as a customer.

What quantity of deals would you be wise to acquire? The overwhelming majority may anticipate holding between ten and twenty stocks.

If you wish to purchase from the London Stock Exchange or the New York Stock Exchange, an intermediary is required. Additionally, they will charge you a fee and frequently work on commission.

What does an offer cost? It fluctuates in response to market demand from buyers and sellers. If demand is significant, costs will also increase.

There are several fees you should be aware of:

- Account fees. This may be delayed depending on the number of trades you conduct.

- Inactivity fees. This could be assessed if your account exceeds the predetermined minimum number of transactions. Because they want you to remain with them, relatively few businesses impose this fee at present.

- Buying or selling. Each time you exchange shares, a fee is assessed.

- Stamp taxation. When purchasing shares, you typically pay a 0.5% transaction fee to the exchange. The only party responsible for payment is the purchaser.

Dividend Investing

This is a method for purchasing dividend-paying securities in order to profit from your investments.

Dividends are payments made by a partnership to its investors. When you own securities that generate profits, you receive a portion of the organization's earnings.

If the company you own stock in has a profit reinvestment plan, you can choose to have your profits reinvested to purchase additional shares rather than receiving them as a dividend.

Regular profit pay is a reliable and secure method of building a nest fund.

Companies that pay out 60% or less of their income as profits are generally safer investments because they are predictable.

Consider organizations that have a history of stable pay and cash flow.

The majority of pay from profits is taxed as common pay, but qualified profit equities held for a longer period (at least 60 days) are taxed at the lower capital increases charge rates.

Bonds

This is the juncture at which a credit is made to an organization or the government. They will provide securities when they need to raise funds to support initiatives.

The primary distinction between a security and a credit is that a security can be traded. There is usually a market where they can be traded. Credits are typically non-transferable arrangements between institutions and customers.

Bonds charge loan fees. The loan fees may be variable or fixed. A security has an expiration date, and when that date arrives, you should receive your money in full.

What is the bond's cost? • The creditworthiness of the person or entity providing the security. The bond is more hazardous the lower its rating. Continuously evaluate the guarantor's track record to determine if they are dependable or hazardous.

• The time remaining until maturity • The interest rate

You can present the attachment to various financial supporters. You are not required to remain with it until its expiration date.

What benefits do bonds offer?

• You are compensated with revenue payments • You receive all the money you contributed if you remain until the end • You can sell it for a profit

What are the downsides?

• Companies can default on their payments to you • If the financing cost decreases, so does the amount of your return

You may observe a security with a higher loan fee, but this indicates that the default risk is higher the higher the financing cost.

Avoid contributing solely based on the advertised financing cost. If the loan fee is high, it indicates the securities are riskier, and you have a greater chance of losing your entire investment.

When financing costs increase, bond prices decline, and vice versa. The loan cost hazard occurs when anticipated interest rates fluctuate. In the event that the loan rate rises, you will be left with a security returning below market rates.

The greater the potential for development, the greater the possibility that interest rates will increase.

There are two methods for generating income by investing in bonds.

The first option is to retain these securities until their maturity date and collect revenue installments. Typically, security premiums are paid twice per year.

The subsequent step is to sell them for a higher price than you initially paid.

You can also invest in security reserves, which are formed when a group of investors combine their funds so that an asset manager can purchase a large number of individual bonds.

There are four fundamental categories of bonds:

- Commercial. They are granted by institutions. Unlike shares, bonds issued by organizations do not confer ownership rights. They are less secure securities, but they typically compensate with higher rates of interest.

- Government bonds. Given by the government agency. It is a method for legislators to raise money without raising taxes. They can be an excellent option for the portfolio's generally secure portion.

- Municipal securities. Presented by cities, states, and counties.

- Agency obligations. Presented by government-affiliated institutions

The market interest rate determines the day-to-day value of an obligation. When selecting bonds, maturity and duration should be considered. Bonds with extended maturities will be significantly more affected by changes in average loan costs. Due to fluctuations in loan costs, securities with extended maturities are subject to a greater degree of risk; consequently, they offer higher yields (respects) and are therefore more attractive to investors.

• Premium. A few organizations assign a FICO score to each security in order to evaluate its quality. The yield decreases as the borrower's FICO score increases.

You can lose money on a security if you sell it before the maturity date for less than what you paid for it, or if the guarantor defaults on payments.

Typically, the duration over which you receive revenue payments from securities is two years.

Due to the fact that they do not all pay at the same time, investing in multiple securities can result in more regular payments.

It is possible to construct a security portfolio yielding monthly income. This can be obtained by purchasing various securities (typically six) that pay a premium on other dates.

Bonds are less susceptible to monetary loss than equities. Therefore, acquiring a few securities and a few equities can reduce portfolio losses. Bonds can be obtained from a number of sources, including investment and commercial institutions, brokers, and corporations.

The minimum investment required to purchase a single security is approximately $1,000, but securities are typically sold in increments of $5,000.

Everyone Can Improve Their Investment Skills.

Permit me to outline my strategy for becoming a better investor. You should perform the few tasks listed below.

Practice, Practice, Practice

There is a proverb that states, "Practice makes man perfect." It means that "persistent practice will enable one to improve in a particular area." The only way to attain a high level of proficiency in any skill is through diligent practice. The more effort you put into something, the better you will become at it. Investing is another skill that improves with practice. Therefore, you must frequently purchase and sell stocks.

WARNING: Do not rehearse with actual cash! There are numerous realistic virtual stock trading systems that enable you to trade real stocks with virtual money at real prices and volumes. Now, anyone can administer a virtual portfolio of one million stocks and practice investing.

Focus on your strengths

If you concentrate on what you're good at and cease doing what you're not, you will improve as an investor.

This is a basic and effective rule for living as well. Most people are unaware of their investing strengths and limitations, so they continually commit the same errors.

Determine your strengths and weaknesses so that you can concentrate on what works and cease doing what does not. How can one determine his or her strengths and weaknesses is the central query.

After gaining an initial understanding of your values, passions, interests, and mission, it's time to take stock of your strengths and vulnerabilities and conduct a straightforward SWOT analysis.

The acronym "SWOT" stands for "Strengths, Weaknesses, Opportunities, and Threats."

Caution is advised before decoding your assets and weaknesses. Do not equate strengths with "good things" and weaknesses with "bad things." Exactly such a value judgment is counterproductive to an effective strategy.

What are your greatest strengths?

Your abilities that consistently generate "positive outcomes" in the tasks you perform are your strengths. For instance, if "organization" is one of your assets, you will find that you are a very organized person when it comes to your finances, managing people, managing resources, etc. Your fortitude will be evident in nearly all of your actions. It is your greatest strength and makes your mind feel very clear and at peace.

Similarly, what are your shortcomings?

They are skills that are not your natural forte, but they manifest in all that you do. For instance, if you struggle with handling numbers, analyzing company balance sheets, analyzing the economic prognosis, and imagining the future, you will have difficulty making investment decisions. You will come to invest in companies with an uncertain future. This is obviously not your strong suit, as your mind becomes hazy and disorganized. The outcomes of your labor will also be subpar.

In the situation described above, reliance is required. One should seek the counsel of someone who is skilled at analysis. You are adept at organizing; you organize your investment portfolio with the assistance of professionals.

Suppose your greatest asset is your patience. This virtue will make you a better investor if you heed the counsel of those who are adept at analyzing the future of companies, the economy, and the markets. Consider that your greatest asset is making quick decisions. Then you can become a successful trader by making quick decisions when your trades begin to incur losses.

Create a squad

No singular investment style or strategy is always successful. Even the greatest investors are exceptional at everything. To consistently outperform the competition, you need a group. When your style or strategy is not functioning in the current market environment, you must pass the baton to someone whose style is effective. The globe is undergoing a rapid transformation. Individuals must adapt to their evolving environments. However, some individuals are unable to adapt and consequently lose all of their past achievements.

Permit me to illustrate Mr. A with a real-world example. From the outset of his career, he remained bullish on the stock market. He amassed a fortune through securities trading. He never shorted a sale. Once Nifty reached 6300 and dropped to 5000, he began accumulating a profit. The market decreased. He continued to increase his plus positions, and the market dropped to 3,700. Once more, he increased his investment in the expectation that the markets will recover. The market reached a new low of 2250. His position indicated that either the stock market or his broker squared off, and he lost everything he had earned over the years. This could have been avoided if he had worked in a team, consulted others, or paid attention to their input. If you are resistant to change, you could receive superior advice from those who are flexible.

Effectiveness Of Passive Income

It is said that automated revenue is compensation for which no effort is required. Occasionally, you may hear it referred to as money you can earn while sleeping. Despite the fact that this is apparent, there is sometimes confusion regarding easy revenue. Infrequently apparent, certain individuals construe this as meaning they will never be required to perform any work for said compensation. It may require a great deal of effort up front to generate automated revenue, including searching for information and instructing yourself to have the option to generate automated revenue. In addition, once you are receiving automated revenue, you will frequently need to perform some support work to maintain the automated revenue flowing.

For instance, you own an investment property and employ a property manager to handle your landlording responsibilities. You will continue to receive income from that investment property without having to deal directly with tenants or septic systems. However, if you allow years to pass and you do not monitor the property manager or occasionally redesign the property, you will likely lose your income. So you end up making money during your downtime because you're not required for the compensation to come in, but that doesn't mean you never have to put effort into the investment.

In addition to establishing up and maintaining the revenue source, automated revenue allows you to collect payment while you sleep. The key is that you receive income even when you're not working. This creates a level of opportunity unknown to the majority.

What would a person's existence be like if they were able to live solely off of automated income, such that they were never required to be present at a specific location to receive pay? Indeed, it can appear as anything the author desires. Examine it. How much time and responsibility are incorporated into your daily work? It's not just the 40+ hours per week that you work that holds you back. Add commute time to the daily hours. Similarly, include preparation and decompression time — the time you spend preparing for work and recuperating from it when you return home. Consider then that your place of residence is entirely dependent on your place of employment. Unless you telecommute, you must reside in close proximity to your place of employment. Consider that 10 to 14 hours of each day are generally devoted to your occupation, and that you are confined to a specific location.

If you do not enjoy your job and where you reside, would you be able to comprehend how much you may be missing out on in your daily life? You have little energy outside of work during the week, and you will be unable to experience a large number of things you enjoy because your position ties you to a specific location.

What does the absence of effort resemble? Imagine that you had sufficient passive income to support your lifestyle so that you did not need to work by any stretch of the imagination. How would your day differ from the 10 to 14 hours devoted to work and the fact that you live far from your favorite activities?

One word: retirement.

Consider what people do when they are resigned. They don't have to get up at a specific time, they can sleep in all day if they want, they can travel whenever they want, they can visit family whenever they want, and they try to do all the things they've always wanted to do but never had the time to do while working.

In the event that all of your pay was inactive, you would actually have this option. When you are able to plan your days exactly how you want because you are not required to be at a specific job, you are experiencing lifestyle design.

Lifestyle configuration entails organizing your life to be precisely what you desire, regardless of the specifics. What types of things would you remember if you had the option to clear your entire schedule for the following week and plan that week to be anything you desired? Here are a few things, some obvious and others more subtle, to keep in mind when designing your own way of life:

residing wherever you choose

dozing in as late as you want

going to bed whenever you choose

watching TV anytime you want

volunteering

pursuing fresh interests

wearing whatever clothing or attire you desire

acquiring new knowledge (e.g., returning to school for a degree that is completely irrelevant).

traveling wherever you desire for as long as you desire.

You can spend time with friends and family whenever you want.

Visiting locations (brunch spots, ski slopes, parks, bars, Disneyland) that are unbearably congested on weekends during the week.

the enumeration continues

If you are currently unattached from a regular job, the world is readily accessible. In all reasonableness, however, not everyone has the goal of achieving complete independence from the rat race, nor will they ever achieve it. For some purposes, automated revenue serves as supplemental compensation. Additional compensation can contribute to financial security, retirement savings, and mental health. Easy income options enable more people to have financial flexibility and security without taking on a second job or adding more responsibilities to their already full schedule. A person with a 40-hour work week, a spouse, and children is unlikely to be able to take on additional employment if they require additional income. However, they could invest in automated revenue speculations and let their cash work for them while they attend to other concerns.

There are entire volumes written on the subject of simple income. A small number of publications discuss the significance of automated revenue. There are numerous publications on the various business standards for automating revenue generation. In addition, a few books, such as The 4-Hour Workweek by Tim Ferriss, meticulously describe the marvel that lifestyle configuration takes into account because of passive income.

There are numerous automated methods to generate income. The key to automatically generating income from land contributions is to grasp the concept of contributing as opposed to working. When you perceive the distinction between contributing and working, you will begin to see the straightforward income options more plainly. There is an entire section about it coming up.

Additionally, the IRS charges unexpectedly for dynamic and automated revenue. Active income, such as that from wholesaling or reselling (because these are active strategies, just as your job is active), is significantly less tax-advantaged than passive income. Automated income tax deductions are so extraordinary that you frequently end up paying nothing in personal taxation because the extensive deductions mitigate for what you would otherwise pay in fees. This may not seem like much, but when you calculate 33% of your income and realize you don't have to pay that to the government, you may suddenly recognize the tax advantage of detached investments. At the time of writing, private investment properties with four units or fewer are the most cost-effective resource class available to investors. As investment properties are regarded as inactive businesses, they qualify for the greatest tax breaks.

No one needs mechanized revenue to be successful. There are a large number of persistently successful individuals who receive a completely dynamic salary. The key is to understand your objectives and have the option to tailor your investments to meet those objectives, which frequently involves the concept of passive income.

The Issue With Savings Accounts

You could use it to store your emergency cash or any currency that requires easy access. It is always prudent to have at least three (or, in a perfect world, around three and a half) and a half years of your income saved for exigencies.

Having a security home will allow you to manage any emergency without the added stress of determining where to obtain the funds. Sometimes, when you make a contribution, your funds will be locked up for a period of time, and you will be unable to withdraw them without incurring fees, which you should avoid in order to limit your losses.

The problem with the bank account is the given loan fees. They are excessively low, which means that any excess funds in your emergency fund are not growing as quickly as they could. There exist speculative opportunities with potentially greater returns.

What exactly is an investment?

It is the point at which you purchase something in order to receive a reward or benefit.

Risk and enterprise go hand in hand. If a venture is generally secure, you should expect low returns, whereas the higher the profits, the greater the risks.

When Should You Make an Investment?

Ideally, you should consider making a contribution once your obligations have been satisfied.

At the very least, when all of your credit obligations are paid in full, when you have amassed a private stash, and when you have a cash reserve account.

Credit obligations carry an exceptionally high premium, so the longer it takes to repay them, the more you owe.

You should also create a savings account for unforeseen emergencies, such as the loss of a job or a serious illness. It should include three to three and a half years' worth of your monthly income.

When you have sufficient funds in your bank account to cover your emergency fund, you are in a position to invest.

How Much Money Is Required To Get Started?

There is no minimum investment amount, but it appears legitimate that you must commence with a few hundred dollars to generate a profit.

Certain investments will have a minimum amount, so always consult with your financial advisor to determine the ideal amount for your situation.

You should also consider the amount of money you are willing to invest. There is always an element of risk, and you should only contribute what you can afford to lose.

Never invest money that you cannot afford to lose. The key is to build up your reserve funds prior to making contributions. Thus, you will have the means to cope with adversities such as job loss or illness.

You should not save money you need to fulfill other obligations.

Consider the Long Term

When you invest, you anticipate greater returns than you would receive from a bank account, but you must confess that you intend to hold your investments for the longer term. Thus, you provide them with the greatest opportunity to reach their destination.

Share prices fluctuate, so a longer holding period affords a greater opportunity for positive events to offset the declines from a bad period.

Being a long-term investor as opposed to a transient merchant enables you to profit from recognizing issues and negotiating solutions. Become increasingly financially astute.

The longer the holding period, the lower the probability of calamity as the base normal return rises.

Investing in the stock market will not result in instantaneous wealth.

Investing in the financial market is a slow, consistent, and reliable method of accumulating wealth. With a normal annual growth rate of 7%, your underlying speculation will double in ten years; however, this will not occur immediately.

The stock market is one of the most effective wealth-building tools available, but you must adhere to a few principles.

You need to know exactly what you are investing in, keep an eye on your expenses, build a diversified portfolio, and contribute for as long as possible if you need the most apparent opportunity to accumulate wealth.

Independent Research

You should understand what you are investing in and how it operates. You can still utilize a financial advisor's services, but it is always preferable to familiarize yourself with everything first.

If you are interested in investing in a specific organization, you should investigate its issues. You can review their financial reports and any other available information about them.

Before undertaking any endeavor, you should conduct your own research.

There are publicly accessible data sources for virtually every industry. The annual report of an organization provides a sufficient overview of the business as well as projections for its future growth.

You can also favor exchange magazines and websites that cater to a particular industry.

Focus on the organization's strengths and weaknesses. Understanding the financial soundness of a company is the most important step in stock analysis.

Learn how to interpret a company's asset report, pay explanation, and income statements.

By learning more about finance, you will realize that you should never blindly accept what stock analysts say, as you should always conduct your own research.

How To Stop Financial Struggle

Adopt a prudent expenditure plan. If you do not know where your money is going or how much you intend to spend on your expenses, it is difficult to manage your finances effectively.

Cut expenses. Recognize where your expenditure is excessive. Assuming you can reduce your expenditure on unnecessary items, you will have more money available for more important tasks, such as paying bills and saving.

Create a rainy day fund. It can help you regain control while maintaining your financial stability. In a perfect environment, you should have three to six months of living expenses saved for emergencies.

Stop creating new responsibilities. Taking care of your debts could free up a substantial amount of money that you could use for other purposes.

Earn additional compensation. There is no limit on the amount of additional income you can acquire. This additional cash may be used for obligation reimbursement, emergency savings, or meeting basic needs.

An Overview of Lifestyle Assets

At this juncture, I have been a full-time land investor for 20 years. Since I can recall, I have been intrigued in land as an investment. I have lived through the Dot-Com bubble and the 9/11 terror attacks, as well as the 2008 Great Recession. As a result of the COVID-19 pandemic, we are presently observing yet another market shift.

My experience has taught me that while no emergency is ever identical, disruption always presents opportunities. The markets have consistently and will continue to expand globally. We must adapt to various market movements by establishing frameworks/equations to avoid risks and capitalize on opportunities in any market condition.

My experience with putting began in the wholesale market in 2000. By 2002, my partner Teresa and I were simultaneously operating a full-time fix-and-flip business and building a portfolio of single-family rentals. During this period, we rehabilitated more than 100 properties and built a small rental portfolio of 27 properties and 51 units. In 2005, Teresa and I had the opportunity to offer luxurious hotel properties to the extremely wealthy. We decided to shutter our fix-and-flip company and sell all of our rental properties.

We had an unlimited budget for three years, jetted around in private luxury aircraft, and spent time with some of the most extraordinary people on the planet, many of whom you would recognize by their first names. In July 2008, Teresa and I made plans to relocate to Newport Beach, California. Due to the ultra-luxurious resort properties we sold, the vast majority of our consumers came from that area or the Manhattan area, and we were planning to relocate our offices to Orange County. We had invested a tremendous amount of effort in Newport and Laguna over the past few years. We fell hopelessly in love with the private community of Crystal Cove, which was an exceptional gated community, and the home had a breathtaking view of the Pacific Ocean. As we made an offer on the house, I sat on the terrace adjacent to the infinity pool and observed dolphins playing in the water.

Missteps To Avoid

Every successful options speculator must endure a learning curve before achieving consistent profits. Some of them spent countless hours reading about the topic or viewing video tutorials in an all-out effort to learn. Others learn at a more leisurely tempo, and once they've mastered the fundamentals, they rely heavily on their own experience. Regardless of the type of learner you are, you can shorten the learning curve by studying the errors of others.

This section outlines six of the most frequent errors made by inexperienced traders that are simple to avoid.

Purchasing Options without Hedging

This is one of the most fundamental errors made by novice options traders, and it is also one of the most costly, as it could result in their immediate bankruptcy.

Purchasing naked options entails purchasing options without any protective trades to cover your investment should the underlying security move against your expectations and harm your trade.

Here Is a Typical Illustration

A trader has a strong belief that a particular stock will rise in the near future and believes he can make a substantial profit by purchasing a few call options, so he proceeds with the purchase. The trader is aware that if the price of the underlying stock rises as anticipated, the potential profits are unlimited, whereas if the price falls, the utmost loss is limited to the amount invested in purchasing the call options.

In theory, the trader's assumption is correct, and it is possible that this particular transaction will be profitable.

In reality, however, it is equally conceivable that the stock will not move as anticipated or may even decline. If the latter occurs, the prices of call options would begin to decline precipitously and may never recover, resulting in significant losses for the trader.

It is nearly impossible to accurately forecast the short-term movement of a stock every time, and a trader who consistently purchases naked options in the hopes of getting lucky is likely to lose much more than he or she gains over the long term.

For a person to generate a profit after purchasing a naked option, the following conditions must be met:

The trader must correctly forecast the movement direction of the underlying stock.

The trajectory of the stock's price movement must be swift enough for the position to be closed before its gains are eroded by time-decay.

The increase in the premium price of the option should also mitigate for any potential decline in implied volatility since the time the option was acquired.

The trader must abandon the position at the optimal time, prior to a reversal of the stock's movement.

Obviously, it is impracticable to expect everything to always fall into place at the same time, which is why naked-options traders frequently lose money even when they correctly predict the movement of the underlying stock.

Despite all of this, many of these traders believe they will fare better in the time that follows a failed trade and repeat their actions until they have lost the majority of their capital and are compelled to stop trading altogether.

My recommendation is to never purchase naked options (unless it is part of a larger strategy to mitigate a position), as the risk is simply not worth it.

Note that while the risk of purchasing naked options is limited to the premium paid, the risk of selling naked options is unlimited and must be avoided unless adequately hedged.

Miscalculating Time-Decay

The second significant error made by novice traders is underestimating time decay.

If you are the buyer of an option and are unable to exit your trade fast, time decay is your worst enemy.

If you are a buyer of call options, you will observe that sometimes, even when the price of the underlying stock rises every day, the price of your call option does not rise or fall. Alternately, if you are a consumer of put options, you may observe that the price of your put option does not increase despite a decline in the price of the underlying stock. Each of these scenarios can be perplexing to someone who is new to options trading.

The aforementioned issues arise when the rate of increase/decrease in the underlying stock's price is insufficient to outpace the rate at which the option's time-value depreciates every day.

To ensure a profitable transaction, an options trader's trading strategy should ideally include a method for countering or minimizing the effect of time-decay, or for making time-decay work in its favor.

Purchasing Options with Significant Implied Volatility

Buying options during periods of high volatility is another frequent error.

During times of high volatility, option premiums can become absurdly overpriced, and if an options trader purchases options during such times, even if the stock moves sharply in accordance with the trader's expectations, a large drop in implied volatility would result in a significant decline in option prices, resulting in losses for the buyer.

On the day that the "Brexit" referendum results were announced, a particular event occurred in my memory. The Nifty index, along with most other global indices such as the Nasdaq 100, fell significantly in response to the outcome, and the volatility index (VIX) increased by over 30%. That day, the option premium for all Nifty options had become absurdly high. However, this increase in volatility was only due to the market's knee-jerk reaction to an unexpected result, and just a couple of days prior, the market had stabilized and begun rising again; the VIX fell significantly, resulting in a corresponding decline in option premium prices.

Traders who purchased options when the VIX was high would have realized their error a day or two earlier when option prices declined, causing them to incur substantial losses as volatility returned to normal levels.

Not Timing Loss Reduction

Wall Street residents have a popular saying: "Cut your losses short and let your winners run."

Even the most seasoned options traders will occasionally make a poor trade. However, what distinguishes them from amateurs is their ability to concede defeat and reduce their losses when necessary. Amateurs hold on to losing trades in the expectation that they will recover, resulting in a larger loss of capital. The experienced traders, who recognize when to concede defeat, withdraw their capital and reinvest it elsewhere.

When trading with a directional strategy and making a wrong decision, it is vital to limit losses as soon as possible. The prudent course of action is to close a losing position if it moves against your expectations and erodes more than 2 to 3 percent of your total capital.

If you are a trader who exclusively employs spread-based strategies, your losses will always be considerably smaller whenever you make an incorrect prediction. When it becomes apparent, however, that the probability of profiting from a trade is too low for whatever reason, it is prudent to cut losses and reinvest in a position with a greater chance of success, rather than crossing one's fingers or praying to a higher power.

Keeping too many of one's eggs in one basket

The experienced players are always aware that they will occasionally lose a trade. They are also aware that they should never place an excessive amount of capital on a single transaction, as a loss could significantly deplete their funds.

For this reason, professionals spread their risk across multiple transactions and allocate no more than 4-5% of their total available capital to a single trade.

Therefore, if you have a total trading capital of $10,000, you should never enter a trade with a maximum potential loss of $500. Following such a practice will ensure that you can endure the occasional loss without significantly depleting your cash reserve. If you fail to adhere to this rule, you may see several months of profits wiped out by a single losing transaction.

Utilizing Brokers Who Charge High Commissions

A dime saved is a dime acquired!

When I first began investing in the stock market many years ago, I paid little heed to the brokerage firm I was using. In any case, I received trading services from one of the largest and most reputable banks in the country, and the brokerage fees levied by my provider were not significantly different from those of other banks that offered comparable services.

Over the years, many discount brokerage firms that charge significantly less began to flourish, but I had not troubled to switch brokers because I was satisfied with my previous one.

Only after quantifying the differences did I recognize that having a low-cost broker made a substantial difference.

If you trade on the Indian Stock Markets, the table below provides a quantitative breakdown of how brokerage fees can eat into your annual earnings if you choose the incorrect broker. The conventional broker in the table below is the bank whose trading services I had previously utilized, whereas the discount broker is the one I use now. For the record, the former is India's third-largest private bank, while the latter is the country's most esteemed discount broker house.

Using a low-cost broker makes a significant difference, particularly when trading a strategy such as the Iron Condor (a relatively low-yield but high-probability strategy), as shown in the table above.

In addition, the annual maintenance fee is higher for a conventional broker, and all of these costs will make a significant difference over time.

Always choose a broker with the lowest possible brokerage, regardless of where in the world you trade, because this will make a difference in the long run. Do a quantitative comparison using a table (similar to the one I used above), and it will be simpler for you to decide which candidate to choose.

Note for Indian Merchants: If you are a trader based in India or if you trade on the Indian Stock Markets, I strongly recommend that you utilize Zerodha, which has been consistently ranked as the top discount broker in the country. I have utilized their services for the past few years and have found them to be exceptional. In addition to having some of the best brokerage rates in the country, they also provide outstanding customer service and maintain an extensive database of articles. Lastly, their trading portal is extremely user-friendly, making order placement swift and painless.

As stated previously, you work hard for your money, so it is reasonable that you want it to grow as much as it possibly can.

You may have both short- and long-term objectives to achieve. Focusing on what needs to be accomplished will lead you in the correct direction.

It is essential to comprehend that if you leave your money in a savings account, you are not making the most of it and may be missing out on genuine opportunities for growth.

Who wouldn't want to increase their income?

You must also achieve a stable financial situation and be able to predict the future. By saving money, you can complete these tasks significantly faster.

Understanding how you can grow your money and the tools available to you is the first move towards a better financial situation and the achievement of your objectives.

No conjecture is devoid of risk. This is something you should adhere to if you wish to increase your financial standing.

There are safer investments with fewer risks than others, and there are high-return investments that require you to accept greater risks. You should carefully observe what you concur with.

Therefore, it is prudent to consult a financial advisor, as he or she will consider your entire financial situation and will want to advise you as to whether the investment you are contemplating is the right one.

That does not mean you should delegate the decisions to someone else. All things considered, it is your money. It is time for you to start learning and understanding about money so that you can make the best decisions for yourself.

Consult a financial consultant, learn about successful financial supporters, conduct your own research, and only then will you be able to determine what is best for you.

Regarding speculation, you can allow your funds to grow and develop additional income-generating opportunities.

Thinking ahead is also essential. Making retirement plans in advance and investing in them will allow you to be in a significantly better position when the time comes. You will not have to rely solely on your State's Pension, which, in most cases, will not be able to provide you with sufficient income to live a pleasant existence.

You must ensure that you have money set aside for your children's college education or to help them ascend the property ladder when they reach adulthood.

Having a plan to leave your family in a secure financial position if something were to happen to you is also something that the overwhelming majority of people attempt to do.

Therefore, investment can have a significant impact on numerous aspects of your life and assist you in achieving your financial objectives. It is an incorrect assumption that only wealthy individuals can contribute. You also have a great deal of available options.

Another advantage of giving is that you may indirectly assist others in certain circumstances, so there's no need to focus solely on your own benefits.

The Issue With Savings Accounts

The bank account plays a significant role, but it is not the only investment option available.

You could use it to store your emergency cash or any currency that requires easy access. It is always prudent to have at least three (or, in a perfect world, around three and a half) and a half years of your income saved for exigencies.

Having a security home will allow you to manage any emergency without the added stress of determining where to obtain the funds. Sometimes, when you make a contribution, your funds will be locked up for a period of time, and you will be unable to withdraw them without incurring fees, which you should avoid in order to limit your losses.

The problem with the bank account is the given loan fees. They are excessively low, which means that any excess funds in your emergency fund are not growing as quickly as they could. There exist speculative opportunities with potentially greater returns.

What exactly is an investment?

It is the point at which you purchase something in order to receive a reward or benefit.

Risk and enterprise go hand in hand. If a venture is generally secure, you should expect low returns, whereas the higher the profits, the greater the risks.

When Should You Make an Investment?

Ideally, you should consider making a contribution once your obligations have been satisfied.

At the very least, when all of your credit obligations are paid in full, when you have amassed a private stash, and when you have a cash reserve account.

Credit obligations carry an exceptionally high premium, so the longer it takes to repay them, the more you owe.

You should also create a savings account for unforeseen emergencies, such as the loss of a job or a serious illness. It should include three to three and a half years' worth of your monthly income.

When you have sufficient funds in your bank account to cover your emergency fund, you are in a position to invest.

www.ingramcontent.com/pod-product-compliance
Lightning Source LLC
Chambersburg PA
CBHW050244120526
44590CB00016B/2210